On Booze

On Booze

·

F. SCOTT FITZGERALD

A NEW DIRECTIONS PEARL

Publisher's Note: The pieces included in *On Booze* were selected from the New
Directions edition of *The Crack-Up*, published originally clothbound in 1945
and as New Directions Paperbook 54 in 1956; reissued as New Directions Paperbook 757 in 1993 and as New Directions Paperbook 1135 in 2009.

Manufactured in the United States of America
New Directions Books are printed on acid-free paper.
First published as a Pearl (NDP1205) by New Directions in 2011
Published simultaneously in Canada by Penguin Books Canada Limited
Design by Erik Rieselbach

Library of Congress Cataloging-in-Publication Data

Fitzgerald, F. Scott (Francis Scott), 1896–1940.
 On booze / F. Scott Fitzgerald.
   p. cm. — (Pearls)
 A collection of F. Scott Fitzgerald's best drinking writings.
 ISBN 978-0-8112-1926-6 (pbk. : alk. paper)
 1. Drinking of alcoholic beverages—Literary collections. I. Title.
PS3511.I9A6 2011
818'.52—dc22

                      2011007596

10 9 8 7 6 5

New Directions Books are published for James Laughlin
by New Directions Publishing Corporation
80 Eighth Avenue, New York, NY 10011

Table of Contents

ON BOOZE

Selections from the Notebooks

¶ "Perfectly respectable girl, but only been drinking that day. No matter how long she lives she'll always know she's killed somebody."

¶ "With a piquant face and all the chic in the world. This is because I was educated in Paris and this in turn I owe to someone's chance remark to Cousin Arletta that she had a nice big daughter who was only twenty-two or three at the time. It took three bromides to calk Cousin Arletta and I started for the Convent of Sacré-Coeur next day."

¶ "We haven't got any more gin," he said. "Will you have a bromide?" he added hopefully.

¶ "Yes mam, if necessary. Look here, you take a girl and she goes into some café where she's got no business to go. Well, then, her escort he gets a little too much to drink an' he goes to sleep an' then some fella comes up and says, 'Hello, sweet mamma,'" or whatever one of those mashers says up here. What does she do? She can't scream, on account of no real lady will scream nowadays—no—she

3

just reaches down in her pocket and slips her fingers into a pair of Powell's defensive brass-knuckles, debutante's size, executes what I call the Society Hook, and Wham! that big fella's on his way to the cellar."

¶ You can order it in four sizes: *demi* (half a litre), *distingué* (one litre), *formidable* (three litres), and *catastrophe* (five litres).

¶ The blurred world seen from a merry-go-round settled into place; the merry-go-round suddenly stopped.

¶ There were only the colleges and the country clubs. The parks were cheerless, without beer and mostly without music. They ended at the monkey house or at some imitation French vista. They were for children—for adults there was nothing.

¶ Debut: the first time a young girl is seen drunk in public.

¶ When he buys his ties he has to ask if gin will make them run.

¶ Max Eastman—like all people with a swaying walk, he seemed to have some secret.

¶ The boy's defence of his mother's innocence in the Lausanne Palace Bar. His mother sleeping with the son of the Consul.

¶ Cocktails before meals like Americans, wines and brandies like Frenchmen, beer like Germans, whiskey-and-soda like the English, and, as they were no longer in the twenties, this preposterous mélange, that was like some gigantic cocktail in a nightmare.

¶ Sir Francis Elliot, King George, the barley water and champagne.

¶ When he gets sober for six months and can't stand any of the people he's liked when drunk.

¶ Sending orchestra second rate champagne—never, *never* do it again.

¶ Lonsdale: "You don't want to drink so much because you'll make a lot of mistakes and develop sensibility and that's a bad trait for business men."

¶ Addresses in his pocket—mostly bootleggers and psychiatrists.

¶ He seldom exuded liquor because now he had tuberculosis and couldn't breathe very freely.

¶ Perhaps a drunk with great bursts of sentimentality or resentment or maudlin grief.

¶ The drunk on *Majestic* and his hundred yard dash.

¶ He went back into the bathroom and swallowed a draught of rubbing alcohol guaranteed to produce violent gastric disturbances.

¶ Two brown port bottles appeared ahead, developed white labels, turned into starched nuns, who seared us with holy eyes as we went by.

¶ When he urinated, it sounded like night prayer.

¶ Drunk at 20, wrecked at 30, dead at 40.
Drunk at 21, human at 31, mellow at 41, dead at 51.

¶ Then I was drunk for many years, and then I died.

Sad Catastrophe

We don't want visitors, we said:
    They come and sit for hours and hours;
They come when we have gone to bed;
    They are imprisoned here by showers;
They come when they are low and bored—
    Drink from the bottle of your heart.
Once it is emptied, the gay horde,
    Shouting the *Rubaiyat*, depart.

I balked: I was at work, I cried;
    Appeared unshaven or not at all;

Was out of gin; the cook had died
    Of small-pox—and more tales as tall.
On boor and friend I turned the same
    Dull eye, the same impatient tone—
The ones with beauty, sense and fame
    Perceived we wished to be alone.

But dull folk, dreary ones and rude—
    Long talker, lonely soul and quack—
Who hereto hadn't dare intrude,
    Found us alone, swarmed to attack,
Thought silence was attention; rage
    An echo of their own home's war—
Glad we had ceased to "be upstage."
    —But the nice people came no more.

Turkey Remains and How to Inter Them with Numerous Scarce Recipes

¶ At this post holiday season, the refrigerators of the nation are overstuffed with large masses of turkey, the sight of which is calculated to give an adult an attack of dizziness. It seems, therefore, an appropriate time to give the owners the benefit of my experience as an old gourmet, in using this surplus material. Some of the recipes have been in the family for generations. (This usually occurs when rigor mortis sets in.) They were collected over years, from old cook books, yellowed diaries of the Pilgrim Fathers, mail order catalogues, golf-bats and trash cans. Not one but has been tried and proven—there are headstones all over America to testify to the fact.

Very well then: here goes:

1. *Turkey Cocktail:* To one large turkey add one gallon of vermouth and a demijohn of angostura bitters. Shake.

...

12. *Turkey with Whiskey Sauce:* This recipe is for a party of four. Obtain a gallon of whiskey, and allow it to age for several hours. Then serve, allowing one quart for each guest. The next day the turkey should be added, little by little, constantly stirring and basting.

—-

¶ "Let's not talk about such things now. I'll tell you something funny instead." Her look was not one of eager anticipation, but he continued, "By merely looking around, you can review the largest battalion of the Boys I've seen collected in one place. This hotel seems to be a clearing house for them—" He returned the nod of a pale and shaky Georgian who sat down at a table across the room. "That young man looks somewhat retired from life. The little devil I came down to see is hopeless. You'd like him—if he comes in, I'll introduce him."

As he was speaking, the flow into the bar began. Nicole's fatigue accepted Dick's ill-advised words and mingled with the fantastic Koran that presently appeared. She saw the males gathered down at the bar: the tall gangling ones; the little pert ones with round thin shoulders; the broad ones with the faces of Nero and Oscar Wilde, or of senators—faces that dissolved suddenly into girlish fatuity, or twisted into leers; the nervous ones who hitched and twitched, jerking open their eyes very wide, and laughed hysterically; the handsome, passive and dumb men who turned their profiles this way and that; the pimply, stodgy men with delicate gestures; or the raw ones with very red lips and frail curly bodies, their shrill voluble tones piping their favorite word "treacherous" above the hot volume of talk; the ones over-self-conscious who glared with eager politeness toward every noise; among them were English types with great racial self-control, Balkan types, one small cooing Siamese. "I think now," Nicole said, "I think I'm going to bed."

"I think so, too."

—Goodby, you unfortunates. Goodby, Hotel of Three Worlds.

TITLES

¶ *Journal of a Pointless Life*
Red and yellow villas, called *Fleur du Bois, Mon Nid,* or *Sans Souci.*

Wore Out His Welcome.
"Your Cake."
Jack a Dull Boy.
Dark Circles.
The Parvenu Hat.
Talks to a Drunk.
The firing of Jasbo Merribo. Sketch.
Tall Women.
Birds in the Bush.
Travels of a Nation.
Don't You Love It?
All Five Senses.
Napoleon's Coat.
Tavern music, Boat trains.
Dated.
Thumbs Up.
The Bed in the Ball Room.
Book of burlesque entitled *These My Betters.*
Title for bad novel: *God's Convict.*
Skin of His Teeth.
Picture-Minded.
Love of a Lifetime.
Gwen Barclay in the Twentieth Century.
Result—Happiness.
Murder of My Aunt.
Police at the Funeral.
The District Eternity.

The Crack-Up

February, 1936

OF COURSE ALL LIFE is a process of breaking down, but the blows that do the dramatic side of the work—the big sudden blows that come, or seem to come, from outside—the ones you remember and blame things on and, in moments of weakness, tell your friends about, don't show their effect all at once. There is another sort of blow that comes from within—that you don't feel until it's too late to do anything about it, until you realize with finality that in some regard you will never be as good a man again. The first sort of breakage seems to happen quick— the second kind happens almost without your knowing it but is realized suddenly indeed.

Before I go on with this short history, let me make a general observation—the test of a first-rate intelligence is the ability to hold two opposed ideas in the mind at the same time, and still retain the ability to function. One should, for example, be able to see that things are hopeless and yet be determined to make them otherwise. This philosophy fitted on to my early adult life, when I saw the improbable, the implausible, often the "impossible," come true. Life was something you dominated if you were any good. Life yielded easily to intelligence and effort, or to what proportion could be mustered of both. It seemed a romantic business to be a successful literary man—you were not ever going to be as famous as a movie star but what note you had was probably longer-lived—you were never going to have the power of a man of strong political or religious convictions but you were certainly more independent. Of course within the practice of your trade you were forever unsatisfied—but I, for one, would not have chosen any other.

As the twenties passed, with my own twenties marching a little ahead of them, my two juvenile regrets—at not being big enough (or good enough) to play football in college, and at not getting overseas during the war—resolved themselves into childish waking dreams of imaginary heroism that were good enough to go to sleep on in restless nights. The big problems of life seemed to solve themselves, and if the business of fixing them was difficult, it made one too tired to think of more general problems.

Life, ten years ago, was largely a personal matter. I must hold in balance the sense of the futility of effort and the sense of the necessity to struggle; the conviction of the inevitability of failure and still the determination to "succeed"—and, more than these, the contradiction between the dead hand of the past and the high intentions of the future. If I could do this through the common ills—domestic, professional and personal—then the ego would continue as an arrow shot from nothingness to nothingness with such force that only gravity would bring it to earth at last.

For seventeen years, with a year of deliberate loafing and resting out in the center—things went on like that, with a new chore only a nice prospect for the next day. I was living hard, too, but: "Up to forty-nine it'll be all right." I said, "I can count on that. For a man who's lived as I have, that's all you could ask."

—And then, ten years this side of forty-nine, I suddenly realized that I had prematurely cracked.

II

Now a man can crack in many ways—can crack in the head—in which case the power of decision is taken from you by others! or in the body, when one can but submit to the white hospital world; or in the nerves. William Seabrook in an unsympathetic book tells, with some pride and a movie ending, of how he became a public charge. What led to his alcoholism or was bound up with it, was a collapse of his nervous system. Though the present writer was not so entangled—having at the time not tasted so much as a glass of beer for six months—it was his nervous reflexes that were giving way—too much anger and too many tears.

Moreover, to go back to my thesis that life has a varying offensive, the realization of having cracked was not simultaneous with a blow, but with a reprieve.

Not long before, I had sat in the office of a great doctor and listened to a grave sentence. With what, in retrospect, seems some equanimity, I had gone on about my affairs in the city where I was then living, not caring much, not thinking how much had been left undone, or what would become of this and that responsibility, like people do in books; I was well insured and anyhow I had been only a mediocre caretaker of most of the things left in my hands, even of my talent.

But I had a strong sudden instinct that I must be alone. I didn't want to see any people at all. I had seen so many people all my life—I was an average mixer, but more than average in a tendency to identify myself, my ideas, my destiny, with those of all classes that I came in contact with. I was always saving or being saved—in a single morning I would go through the emotions ascribable to Wellington at Waterloo. I lived in a world of inscrutable hostiles and inalienable friends and supporters.

But now I wanted to be absolutely alone and so arranged a certain insulation from ordinary cares.

It was not an unhappy time. I went away and there were fewer people. I found I was good-and-tired. I could lie around and was glad to, sleeping or dozing sometimes twenty hours a day and in the intervals trying resolutely not to think—instead I made lists—made lists and tore them up, hundreds of lists: of cavalry leaders and football players and cities, and popular tunes and pitchers, and happy times, and hobbies and houses lived in and how many suits since I left the army and how many pairs of shoes (I didn't count the suit I bought in Sorrento that shrunk, nor the pumps and dress shirt and collar that I carried around for years and never wore, because the pumps got damp and grainy and the shirt and collar got yellow and starch-rotted). And lists of women I'd liked, and of the times I had let myself be snubbed by people who had not been my betters in character or ability.

—And then suddenly, surprisingly, I got better.

—And cracked like an old plate as soon as I heard the news.

That is the real end of this story. What was to be done about it will have to rest in what used to be called the "womb of time." Suffice it to say that after about an hour of solitary pillow-hugging, I began to realize that for two years my life had been a drawing on resources that I did not possess, that I had been mortgaging myself physically and spiritually up to the hilt. What was the small gift of life given back in comparison to that?—when there had once been a pride of direction and a confidence in enduring independence.

I realized that in those two years, in order to preserve something—an inner hush maybe, maybe not—I had weaned myself from all the things I used to love—that every act of life from the morning tooth-brush to the friend at dinner had become an effort. I saw that for a long time I had not liked people and things, but only followed the rickety old pretense of liking. I saw that even my love for those closest to me was become only an attempt to love, that my casual relations—with an editor, a tobacco seller, the child of a friend, were only what I remembered I *should* do, from other days. All in the same month I became bitter about such things as the sound of the radio, the advertisements in the magazines, the screech of tracks, the dead silence of the country—contemptuous at human softness, immediately (if secretively) quarrelsome toward hardness—hating the night when I couldn't sleep and hating the day because it went toward night. I slept on the heart side now because I knew that the sooner I could tire that out, even a little, the sooner would come that blessed hour of nightmare which, like a catharsis, would enable me to better meet the new day.

There were certain spots, certain faces I could look at. Like most Middle Westerners, I have never had any but the vaguest race prejudices—I always had a secret yen for the lovely Scandinavian blondes who sat on porches in St. Paul but hadn't emerged enough economically to be part of what was then society. They were too nice to be "chickens" and too quickly off the farmlands to seize a place in the sun, but I remember going round blocks to catch a single glimpse of shining hair—the bright shock of a girl I'd never know. This is urban, unpopular talk. It strays afield from the fact that in these latter days I couldn't stand the sight of Celts, English, Politicians, Strangers, Virginians, Negroes (light or dark), Hunting People, or retail clerks, and middlemen in general, all writers (I avoided writers very carefully because they can perpetuate trouble as no one else can)—and all the classes as classes and most of them as members of their class ...

Trying to cling to something, I liked doctors and girl children up to the age of about thirteen and well-brought-up boy children from about eight years old on. I could have peace and happiness with these few categories of people. I forgot to add that I liked old men—men over seventy, sometimes over sixty if their faces looked seasoned. I liked Katharine Hepburn's face on the screen, no matter what was said about her pretentiousness, and Miriam Hopkins' face, and old friends if I only saw them once a year and could remember their ghosts.

All rather inhuman and undernourished, isn't it? Well, that, children, is the true sign of cracking up.

It is not a pretty picture. Inevitably it was carted here and there within its frame and exposed to various critics. One of them can only be described as a person whose life makes other people's lives seem like death—even this time when she was cast in the usually unappealing role of Job's comforter. In spite of the fact that this story is over, let me append our conversation as a sort of postscript:

"Instead of being so sorry for yourself, listen—" she said. (She always says "Listen," because she thinks while she talks—*really* thinks.) So she said: "Listen. Suppose this wasn't a crack in you—suppose it was a crack in the Grand Canyon."

"The crack's in me," I said heroically.

"Listen! The world only exists in your eyes—your conception of it. You can make it as big or as small as you want to. And you're trying to be a little puny individual. By God, if I ever cracked, I'd try to make the world crack with me. Listen! The world only exists through your apprehension of it, and so it's much better to say that it's not you that's cracked—it's the Grand Canyon."

"Baby et up all her Spinoza?"

"I don't know anything about Spinoza. I know—" She spoke, then, of old woes of her own, that seemed, in the telling, to have been more dolorous than mine, and how she had met them, over-ridden them, beaten them.

I felt a certain reaction to what she said, but I am a slow-thinking man, and it occurred to me simultaneously that of all natural forces, vitality is the incommunicable one. In days when juice came into one as an article without duty, one tried to distribute it—but always without success; to further mix metaphors, vitality never "takes." You have it or you haven't it, like health or brown eyes or honor or a baritone voice. I might have asked some of it from her, neatly wrapped and ready for home cooking and digestion, but I could never have got it—not if I'd waited around for a thousand hours with the tin cup of self-pity. I could walk from her door, holding myself very carefully like cracked crockery, and go away into the world of bitterness, where I was making a home with such materials as are found there—and quote to myself after I left her door:

"Ye are the salt of the earth. But if the salt hath lost its savour, wherewith shall it be salted?"

Matthew 5-13.

PASTING IT TOGETHER

March, 1936

In a previous article this writer told about his realization that what he had before him was not the dish that he had ordered for his forties. In fact—since he and the dish were one, he described himself as a cracked plate, the kind that one wonders whether it is worth preserving. Your editor thought that the article suggested too many aspects without regarding them closely, and probably many readers felt the same way—and there are always those to whom all self-revelation is contemptible, unless it ends with a noble thanks to the gods for the Unconquerable Soul.

But I had been thanking the gods too long, and thanking them for nothing. I wanted to put a lament into my record, without even the background of the Euganean Hills to give it color. There weren't any Euganean hills that I could see.

Sometimes, though, the cracked plate has to be retained in the pantry, has to be kept in service as a household necessity. It can never again be warmed on the stove nor shuffled with the other plates in the dishpan; it will not be brought out for company, but it will do to hold crackers late at night or to go into the ice box under left-overs...

Hence this sequel—a cracked plate's further history.

Now the standard cure for one who is sunk is to consider those in actual destitution or physical suffering—this is an all-weather beatitude for gloom in general and fairly salutory day-time advice for everyone. But at three o'clock in the morning, a forgotten package has the same tragic importance as a death sentence, and the cure doesn't work—and in a real dark night of the soul it is always three o'clock in the morning, day after day. At that hour the tendency is to refuse to face things as long as possible by retiring into an infantile dream—but one is continually startled out of this by various contacts with the world. One meets these occasions as quickly and carelessly as possible and retires once more back into the dream, hoping that things will adjust themselves by some great material or spiritual bonanza. But as the withdrawal persists there is less and less chance of the bonanza— one is not waiting for the fade-out of a single sorrow, but rather being an unwilling witness of an execution, the disintegration of one's own personality . . .

Unless madness or drugs or drink come into it, this phase comes to a dead-end, eventually, and is succeeded by a vacuous quiet. In this you can try to estimate what has been sheared away and what is left. Only when this quiet came to me, did I realize that I had gone through two parallel experiences.

The first time was twenty years ago, when I left Princeton in junior year with a complaint diagnosed as malaria. It transpired, through an X-ray taken a dozen years later, that it had been tuberculosis—a mild case, and after a few months of rest I went back to college. But I had lost certain offices, the chief one was the presidency of the Triangle Club, a musical comedy idea, and also I dropped back a class. To me college would never be the same. There were to be no badges of pride, no medals, after all. It seemed on one March afternoon that I had lost every single thing I wanted—and that night was the first time that I hunted down the spectre of womanhood that, for a little while, makes everything else seem unimportant.

Years later I realized that my failure as a big shot in college was all right—instead of serving on committees, I took a beating on English poetry; when I got the idea of what it was all about, I set about learning how to write. On Shaw's principle that "If you don't get what you like, you better like what you get," it was a lucky break—at the moment it was a harsh and bitter business to know that my career as a leader of men was over.

Since that day I have not been able to fire a bad servant, and I am astonished and impressed by people who can. Some old desire for personal dominance was broken and gone. Life around me was a solemn dream, and I lived on the letters I wrote to a girl in another city. A man does not recover from such jolts—he becomes a different person and, eventually, the new person finds new things to care about.

The other episode parallel to my current situation took place after the war, when I had again over-extended my flank. It was one of those tragic loves doomed for lack of money, and one day the girl closed it out on the basis of common sense. During a long summer of despair I wrote a novel instead of letters, so it came out all right, but it came out all right for a different person. The man with the jingle of money in his pocket who married the girl a year later would always cherish an abiding distrust, an animosity, toward the leisure class—not the conviction of a revolutionist but the smouldering hatred of a peasant. In the years since then I have never been able to stop wondering where my friends' money came from, nor to stop thinking that at one time a sort of *droit de seigneur* might have been exercised to give one of them my girl.

For sixteen years I lived pretty much as this latter person, distrusting the rich, yet working for money with which to share their mobility and the grace that some of them brought into their lives. During this time I had plenty of the usual horses shot from under me—I remember some of their names—*Punctured Pride, Thwarted Expectation, Faithless, Show-off, Hard Hit, Never Again*. And after awhile I wasn't twenty-five, then not even thirty-five, and nothing was quite as good. But in all these years I don't remember a moment of discouragement. I saw honest men through moods of suicidal gloom—some of them gave up and died; others adjusted themselves and went on to a larger success than mine; but my morale never sank below the level of self-disgust when I had put on some unsightly personal show. Trouble has no necessary connection with discouragement—discouragement has a germ of its own, as different from trouble as arthritis is different from a stiff joint.

When a new sky cut off the sun last spring, I didn't at first relate it to what had happened fifteen or twenty years ago. Only gradually did a certain family resemblance come through—an over-extension of the flank, a burning of the candle at both ends; a call upon physical resources that I did not command, like a man over-drawing at his bank. In its impact this blow was more violent than the other two but it was the same in kind—a feeling that I was standing at twilight on a deserted range, with an empty rifle in my hands and the targets down. No problem set— simply a silence with only the sound of my own breathing.

In this silence there was a vast irresponsibility toward every obligation, a deflation of all my values. A passionate belief in order, a disregard of motives or consequences in favor of guess work and prophecy, a feeling that craft and industry would have a place in any world—one by one, these and other convictions were swept away. I saw that the novel, which at my maturity was the strongest and supplest medium for conveying thought and emotion from one human being to another, was becoming subordinated to a mechanical and communal art that, whether in the hands of Hollywood merchants or Russian idealists, was capable of reflecting only the tritest thought, the most obvious emotion. It was an art in which words were subordinate to images, where personality was worn down to the inevitable low gear of collaboration. As long past as 1930, I had a hunch that the talkies would make even the best selling novelist as archaic as silent pictures. People still read, if only Professor Canby's book of the month— curious children nosed at the slime of Mr. Tiffany Thayer in the drugstore libraries—but there was a rankling indignity, that to me had become almost an obsession, in seeing the power of the written word subordinated to another power, a more glittering, a grosser power ...

I set that down as an example of what haunted me during the long night—this was something I could neither accept nor struggle against, something which tended to make my efforts obsolescent, as the chain stores have crippled the small merchant, an exterior force, unbeatable—

(I have the sense of lecturing now, looking at a watch on the desk before me and seeing how many more minutes—).

Well, when I had reached this period of silence, I was forced into a measure that no one ever adopts voluntarily: I was impelled to think. God, was it difficult! The moving about of great secret trunks. In the first exhausted halt, I wondered whether I had ever thought. After a long time I came to these conclusions, just as I write them here:

(1) That I had done very little thinking, save within the problems of my craft. For twenty years a certain man had been my intellectual conscience. That was Edmund Wilson.

(2) That another man represented my sense of the "good life," though I saw him once in a decade, and since then he might have been hung. He is in the fur business in the Northwest and wouldn't like his name set down here. But in difficult situations I had tried to think what *he* would have thought, how *he* would have acted.

(3) That a third contemporary had been an artistic conscience to me—I had not imitated his infectious style, because my own style, such as it is, was formed before he published anything, but there was an awful pull toward him when I was on a spot.

(4) That a fourth man had come to dictate my relations with other people when these relations were successful: how to do, what to say. How to make people at least momentarily happy (in opposition to Mrs. Post's theories of how to make everyone thoroughly uncomfortable with a sort of systematized vulgarity). This always confused me and made me want to go out and get drunk, but this man had seen the game, analyzed it and beaten it, and his word was good enough for me.

(5) That my political conscience had scarcely existed for ten years save as an element of irony in my stuff. When I became again concerned with the system I should function under, it was a man much younger than myself who brought it to me, with a mixture of passion and fresh air.

So there was not an "I" any more—not a basis on which I could organize my self-respect—save my limitless capacity for toil that it seemed I possessed no more. It was strange to have no self—to be like a little boy left alone in a big house, who knew that now he could do anything he wanted to do, but found that there was nothing that he wanted to do—

(The watch is past the hour and I have barely reached my thesis. I have some doubts as to whether this is of general interest, but if anyone wants more there is plenty left, and your editor will tell me. If you've had enough, say so— but not too loud, because I have the feeling that someone, I'm not sure who, is sound asleep—someone who could have helped me to keep my shop open. It wasn't Lenin, and it wasn't God.)

F. Scott Fitzgerald

HANDLE WITH CARE

April, 1936

I have spoken in these pages of how an exceptionally optimistic young man experienced a crack-up of all values, a crack-up that he scarcely knew of until long after it occurred. I told of the succeeding period of desolation and of the necessity of going on, but without benefit of Henley's familiar heroics, "my head is bloody but unbowed." For a check-up of my spiritual liabilities indicated that I had no particular head to be bowed or unbowed. Once I had had a heart but that was about all I was sure of.

This was at least a starting place out of the morass in which I floundered: "I felt—therefore I was." At one time or another there had been many people who had leaned on me, come to me in difficulties or written me from afar, believed implicitly in my advice and my attitude toward life. The dullest platitude monger or the most unscrupulous Rasputin who can influence the destinies of many people must have some individuality, so the question became one of finding why and where I had changed, where was the leak through which, unknown to myself, my enthusiasm and my vitality had been steadily and prematurely trickling away.

One harassed and despairing night I packed a briefcase and went off a thousand miles to think it over. I took a dollar room in a drab little town where I knew no one and sunk all the money I had with me in a stock of potted meat, crackers and apples. But don't let me suggest that the change from a rather overstuffed world to a comparative asceticism was any Research Magnificent—I only wanted absolute quiet to think out why I had developed a sad attitude toward sadness, a melancholy attitude toward melancholy and a tragic attitude toward tragedy—*why I had become identified with the objects of my horror or compassion.*

Does this seem a fine distinction? It isn't: identification such as this spells the death of accomplishment. It is something like this that keeps insane people from working. Lenin did not willingly endure the sufferings of his proletariat, nor Washington of his troops, nor Dickens of his London poor. And when Tolstoy tried some such merging of himself with the objects of his attention, it was a fake and a failure. I mention these because they are the men best known to us all.

It was dangerous mist. When Wordsworth decided that "there had passed away a glory from the earth," he felt no compulsion to pass away with it, and the Fiery Particle Keats never ceased his struggle gainst t. b. nor in his last moments relinquished his hope of being among the English poets.

My self-immolation was something sodden-dark. It was very distinctly not modern—yet I saw it in others, saw it in a dozen men of honor and industry since the war. (I heard you, but that's too easy—there were Marxians among these men.) I had stood by while one famous contemporary of mine played with the idea of the Big Out for half a year; I had watched when another, equally eminent, spent months in an asylum unable to endure any contact with his fellow men. And of those who had given up and passed on I could list a score.

This led me to the idea that the ones who had survived had made some sort of clean break. This is a big word and is no parallel to a jail-break when one is probably headed for a new jail or will be forced back to the old one. The famous "Escape" or "run away from it all" is an excursion in a trap even if the trap includes the south seas, which are only for those who want to paint them or sail them. A clean break is something you cannot come back from; that is irretrievable because it makes the past cease to exist. So, since I could no longer fulfill the obligations that life had set for me or that I had set for myself, why not slay the empty shell who had been posturing at it for four years? I must continue to be a writer because that was my only way of life, but I would cease any attempts to be a person—to be kind, just or generous. There were plenty of counterfeit coins around that would pass instead of these and I knew where I could get them at a nickel on the dollar. In thirty-nine years an observant eye has learned to detect where the milk is watered and the sugar is sanded, the rhinestone passed for diamond and the stucco for stone. There was to be no more giving of myself—all giving was to be outlawed henceforth under a new name, and that name was Waste.

The decision made me rather exuberant, like anything that is both real and new. As a sort of beginning there was a whole shaft of letters to be tipped into the waste basket when I went home, letters that wanted something for nothing—to read this man's manuscript, market this man's poem, speak free on the radio, indite notes of introduction, give this interview, help with the plot of this play, with this domestic situation, perform this act of thoughtfulness or charity.

The conjuror's hat was empty. To draw things out of it had long been a sort of sleight of hand, and now, to change the metaphor, I was off the dispensing end of the relief roll forever.

The heady villainous feeling continued.

I felt like the beady-eyed men I used to see on the commuting train from Great Neck fifteen years back—men who didn't care whether the world tumbled into chaos tomorrow if it spared their houses. I was one with them now, one with the smooth articles who said:

"I'm sorry but business is business." Or:

"You ought to have thought of that before you got into this trouble." Or:

"I'm not the person to see about that."

And a smile—ah, I would get me a smile. I'm still working on that smile. It is to combine the best qualities of a hotel manager, an experienced old social weasel, a headmaster on visitors' day, a colored elevator man, a pansy pulling a profile, a producer getting stuff at half its market value, a trained nurse coming on a new job, a body-vender in her first rotogravure, a hopeful extra swept near the camera, a ballet dancer with an infected toe, and of course the great beam of loving kindness common to all those from Washington to Beverly Hills who must exist by virtue of the contorted pan.

The voice too—I am working with a teacher on the

voice. When I have perfected it the larynx will show no ring of conviction except the conviction of the person I am talking to. Since it will be largely called upon for the elicitation of the word "Yes," my teacher (a lawyer) and I are concentrating on that, but in extra hours. I am learning to bring into it that polite acerbity that makes people feel that far from being welcome they are not even tolerated and are under continual and scathing analysis at every moment. These times will of course not coincide with the smile. This will be reserved exclusively for those from whom I have nothing to gain, old worn-out people or young struggling people. They won't mind—what the hell, they get it most of the time anyhow.

But enough. It is not a matter of levity. If you are young and you should write asking to see me and learn how to be a sombre literary man writing pieces upon the state of emotional exhaustion that often overtakes writers in their prime—if you should be so young and so fatuous as to do this, I would not do so much as acknowledge your letter, unless you were related to someone very rich and important indeed. And if you were dying of starvation outside my window, I would go out quickly and give you the smile and the voice (if no longer the hand) and stick around till somebody raised a nickel to phone for the ambulance, that is if I thought there would be any copy in it for me.

I have now at last become a writer only. The man I had persistently tried to be became such a burden that I have "cut him loose" with as little compunction as a Negro lady cuts loose a rival on Saturday night. Let the good people function as such—let the overworked doctors die in harness with one week's "vacation" a year that they can devote to straightening out their family affairs, and let the underworked doctors scramble for cases at one dollar a throw; let the soldiers be killed and enter immediately into the Valhalla of their profession. That is their contract with the gods. A writer need have no such ideals unless he makes them for himself, and this one has quit. The old dream of being an entire man in the Goethe-Byron-Shaw tradition, with an opulent American touch, a sort of combination of J. P. Morgan, Topham Beauclerk and St. Francis of Assisi, has been relegated to the junk heap of the shoulder pads worn for one day on the Princeton freshman football field and the overseas cap never worn overseas.

So what? This is what I think now: that the natural state of the sentient adult is a qualified unhappiness. I think also that in an adult the desire to be finer in grain than you are, "a constant striving" (as those people say who gain their bread by saying it) only adds to this unhappiness in the end—that end that comes to our youth and hope. My own happiness in the past often approached such an ecstasy that I could not share it even with the person dearest to me but had to walk it away in quiet streets and lanes with only fragments of it to distil into little lines in books—and I think that my happiness, or talent for self-delusion or what you will, was an exception. It was not the natural thing but the unnatural—unnatural as the Boom; and my recent experience parallels the wave of despair that swept the nation when the Boom was over.

I shall manage to live with the new dispensation, though it has taken some months to be certain of the fact. And just as the laughing stoicism which has enabled the American Negro to endure the intolerable conditions of his existence has cost him his sense of the truth—so in my case there is a price to pay. I do not any longer like the postman, nor the grocer, nor the editor, nor the cousin's husband, and he in turn will come to dislike me, so that life will never be very pleasant again, and the sign *Cave Canem* is hung permanently just above my door. I will try to be a correct animal though, and if you throw me a bone with enough meat on it I may even lick your hand.

"Show Mr and Mrs. F. to Number—"

May–June, 1934

WE ARE MARRIED. The Sibylline parrots are protesting the sway of the first bobbed heads in the Biltmore panelled luxe. The hotel is trying to look older.

The faded rose corridors of the Commodore end in subways and subterranean metropolises—a man sold us a broken Marmon and a wild burst of friends spent half an hour revolving in the revolving door.

There were lilacs open to the dawn near the boarding house in Westport where we sat up all night to finish a story. We quarreled in the gray morning dew about morals; and made up over a red bathing suit.

The Manhattan took us in one late night though we looked very young and gay. Ungratefully we packed the empty suitcase with spoons and the phone book and a big square pin-cushion.

The Traymore room was gray and the chaise longue big enough for a courtesan. The sound of the sea kept us awake.

Electric fans blew the smell of peaches and hot biscuit and the cindery aroma of travelling salesmen through the New Willard halls in Washington.

But the Richmond hotel had a marble stair and long un-opened rooms and marble statues of the gods lost somewhere in its echoing cells.

At the O. Henry in Greensville they thought a man and his wife ought not to be dressed alike in white knicker-bockers in nineteen-twenty and we thought the water in the tubs ought not to run red mud.

Next day the summer whine of phonographs billowed out the skirts of the southern girls in Athens. There were so many smells in the drug stores and so much organdy and so many people just going somewhere ... We left at dawn.

1921

They were respectful in the Cecil in London; disciplined by the long majestuous twilights on the river and we were young but we were impressed anyway by the Hindus and the Royal Processions.

At the St. James and Albany in Paris we smelled up the room with an uncured Armenian goat-skin and put the unmelting "ice-cream" outside the window, and there were dirty postcards, but we were pregnant.

The Royal Danieli in Venice had a gambling machine and the wax of centuries over the window-sill and there were fine officers on the American destroyer. We had fun in a gondola feeling like a soft Italian song.

Bamboo curtains and an asthma patient complaining

of the green plush and an ebony piano were all equally embalmed in the formal parlors of the Hôtel d'Italie in Florence.

But there were fleas on the gilded filigree of the Grand Hôtel in Rome; men from the British embassy scratched behind the palms; the clerks said it was the flea season.

Claridge's in London served strawberries in a gold dish, but the room was an inside room and gray all day, and the waiter didn't care whether we left or not, and he was our only contact.

In the fall we got to the Commodore in St. Paul, and while leaves blew up the streets we waited for our child to be born.

1922–1923

The Plaza was an etched hotel, dainty and subdued, with such a handsome head waiter that he never minded lending five dollars or borrowing a Rolls-Royce. We didn't travel much in those years.

1924

The Deux Mondes in Paris ended about a blue abysmal court outside our window. We bathed the daughter in the *bidet* by mistake and she drank the gin fizz thinking it was lemonade and ruined the luncheon table next day.

Goat was to eat in Grimm's Park Hotel in Hyères, and the bougainvillea was brittle as its own color in the hot white dust. Many soldiers loitered outside the gardens and brothels listening to the nickelodeons. The nights, smelling of honeysuckle and army leather, staggered up the mountain side and settled upon Mrs. Edith Wharton's garden.

At the Ruhl in Nice we decided on a room not facing the sea, on all the dark men being princes, on not being able to afford it even out of season. During dinner on the terrace, stars fell in our plates, and we tried to identify ourselves with the place by recognizing faces from the boat. But nobody passed and we were alone with the deep blue grandeur and the *filet de sole Ruhl* and the second bottle of champagne.

The Hôtel de Paris at Monte Carlo was like a palace in a detective story. Officials got us things: tickets and permissions, maps and newly portentous identities. We waited a good while in the formalized sun while they fitted us out with all we needed to be fitting guests of the Casino. Finally, taking control of the situation, we authoritatively sent the bell-boy for a tooth-brush.

Wistaria dripped in the court of the Hôtel d'Europe at Avignon and the dawn rumbled up in market carts. A lone lady in tweeds drank Martinis in the dingy bar. We met French friends at the Taverne Riche and listened to the bells of late afternoon reverberate along the city walls. The Palace of the Popes rose chimerically through the gold end of day over the broad still Rhône, while we did nothing, assiduously, under the plane trees on the opposite bank.

Like Henri IV, a French patriot fed his babies red wine in the Continental at St. Raphaël and there were no carpets because of summer, so echoes of the children's protestations fell pleasantly amidst the clatter of dishes and china. By this time we could identify a few words of French and felt ourselves part of the country.

The Hôtel du Cap at Antibes was almost deserted. The heat of day lingered in the blue and white blocks of the balcony and from the great canvas mats our friends had spread along the terrace we warmed our sunburned backs and invented new cocktails.

The Miramare in Genoa festooned the dark curve of the shore with garlands of lights, and the shape of the hills was picked out of the darkness by the blaze from the windows of high hotels. We thought of the men parading the gay arcades as undiscovered Carusos but they all assured us that Genoa was a business city and very like America and Milan.

We got to Pisa in the dark and couldn't find the leaning tower until we passed it by accident leaving the Royal Victoria on our way out. It stood stark in a field by itself. The Arno was muddy and not half as insistent as it is in the cross-word puzzles.

Marion Crawford's mother died in the Quirinal Hotel at Rome. All the chamber-maids remember it and tell the visitors about how they spread the room with newspapers afterwards. The sitting-rooms are hermetically sealed and palms conceal the way to open the windows. Middle-aged English doze in the stale air and nibble stale-salted peanuts with the hotel's famous coffee, which comes out of a calliope-like device for filling it full of grounds, like the glass balls that make snow storms when shaken.

In the Hôtel des Princes at Rome we lived on Bel Paese cheese and Corvo wine and made friends with a delicate spinster who intended to stop there until she finished a three-volume history of the Borgias. The sheets were damp and the nights were perforated by the snores of the people next door, but we didn't mind because we could always come home down the stairs to the Via Sistina, and there were jonquils and beggars along that way. We were too superior at that time to use the guide books and wanted to discover the ruins for ourselves, which we did when we had exhausted the night-life and the market places and the campagna. We liked the Castello Sant'Angelo because of its round mysterious unity and the river and the debris about its base. It was exciting being lost between centuries in the Roman dusk and taking your sense of direction from the Colosseum.

1925

At the hotel in Sorrento we saw the tarantella, but it was a *real* one and we had seen so many more imaginative adaptations....

A southern sun drugged the court of the Quisisana to somnolence. Strange birds protested their sleepiness beneath the overwhelming cypress while Compton Mackenzie told us why he lived in Capri: Englishmen must have an island.

The Tiberio was a high white hotel scalloped about the base by the rounded roofs of Capri, cupped to catch rain which never falls. We climbed to it through devious dark alleys that house the island's Rembrandt butcher shops and bakeries; then we climbed down again to the dark pagan hysteria of Capri's Easter, the resurrection of the spirit of the people.

When we got back to Marseilles, going north again, the streets about the waterfront were bleached by the brightness of the harbor and pedestrians gayly discussed errors of time at little cafés on the corner. We were so damn glad of the animation.

The hotel in Lyons wore an obsolete air and nobody ever heard of Lyonnaise potatoes and we became so discouraged with touring that we left the little Renault there and took the train for Paris.

The Hôtel Florida had catacornered rooms; the gilt had peeled from the curtain fixtures.

When we started out again after a few months, touring south, we slept six in a room in Dijon (Hôtel du Dump, Pens. from 2 frs. Pouring water) because there wasn't any other place. Our friends considered themselves somewhat compromised but snored towards morning.

In Salies-de-Béarn in the Pyrenees we took a cure for colitis, disease of that year, and rested in a white pine room in the Hôtel Bellevue, flush with thin sun rolled down from the Pyrenees. There was a bronze statue of Henri IV on the mantel in our room, for his mother was born there. The boarded windows of the Casino were splotched with bird droppings—along the misty streets we bought canes with spears on the end and were a little discouraged about everything. We had a play on Broadway and the movies offered $60,000, but we were china people by then and it didn't seem to matter particularly.

When that was over, a hired limousine drove us to Toulouse, careening around the grey block of Carcassonne and through the long unpopulated planes of the Cote d'Argent. The Hôtel Tivollier, though ornate, had fallen into disuse. We kept ringing for the waiter to assure ourselves that life went on somewhere in the dingy crypt. He appeared resentfully and finally we induced him to give us so much beer that it heightened the gloom.

In the Hôtel O'Connor old ladies in white lace rocked their pasts to circumspection with the lullabyic motion of the hotel chairs. But they were serving blue twilights at the cafés along the Promenade des Anglais for the price of a porto, and we danced their tangos and watched girls shiver in the appropriate clothes for the Côte d'Azur. We went to the Perroquet with friends, one of us wearing a blue hyacinth and the other an ill temper which made him buy a wagon full of roasted chestnuts and immediately scatter their warm burnt odor like largesse over the cold spring night.

In the sad August of that year we made a trip to Mentone, ordering bouillabaisse in an aquarium-like pavillion by the sea across from the Hôtel Victoria. The hills were silver-olive, and of the true shape of frontiers.

Leaving the Riviera after a third summer, we called on a writer friend at the Hôtel Continental at Cannes. He was proud of his independence in adopting a black mongrel dog. He had a nice house and a nice wife and we envied his comfortable installations that gave the effect of his having retired from the world when he had really taken such of it as he wanted and confined it.

When we got back to America we went to the Roosevelt Hotel in Washington and to see one of our mothers. The cardboard hotels, bought in sets, made us feel as if we committed a desecration by living in them—we left the brick pavements and the elms and the heterogeneous qualities of Washington and went further south.

1927

It takes so long to get to California, and there were so many nickel handles, gadgets to avoid, buttons to invoke, and such a lot of newness and Fred Harvey, that when one of us thought he had appendicitis we got out at El Paso. A cluttered bridge dumps one in Mexico where the restaurants are trimmed with tissue paper and there are contraband perfumes—we admired the Texas rangers, not having seen men with guns on their hips since the war.

We reached California in time for an earthquake. It was sunny, and misty at night. White roses swung luminous in the mist from a trellis outside the Ambassador windows; a bright exaggerated parrot droned incomprehensible shouts in an aquamarine pool—of course everybody interpreted them to be obscenities; geraniums underscored the discipline of the California flora. We paid homage to the pale aloof concision of Diana Manners' primitive beauty and dined at Pickfair to marvel at Mary Pickford's dynamic subjugation of life. A thoughtful limousine carried us for California hours to be properly moved by the fragility of Lillian Gish, too aspiring for life, clinging vine-like to occultisms.

From there we went to the DuPont in Wilmington. A friend took us to tea in the mahogany recesses of an almost feudal estate, where the sun gleamed apologetically in the silver tea-service and there were four kinds of buns and four indistinguishable daughters in riding clothes and a mistress of the house too busily preserving the charm of another era to separate out the children. We leased a very big old mansion on the Delaware River. The squareness of the rooms and the sweep of the columns were to bring us a judicious tranquility. There were sombre horse-chestnuts in the yard and a white pine bending as graciously as a Japanese brush drawing.

We went up to Princeton. There was a new colonial inn, but the campus offered the same worn grassy parade ground for the romantic spectres of Light-Horse Harry Lee and Aaron Burr. We loved the temperate shapes of Nassau Hall's old brick, and the way it seems still a tribunal of early American ideals, the elm walks and meadows, the college windows open to the spring—open, open to everything in life—for a minute.

The Negroes are in knee-breeches at the Cavalier in Virginia Beach. It is theatrically southern and its newness is a bit barren, but there is the best beach in America; at that time, before the cottages were built, there were dunes and the moon tripped, fell, in the sandy ripples along the sea-front.

Next time we went, lost and driven now like the rest, it was a free trip north to Quebec. They thought maybe we'd write about it. The Château Frontenac was built of toy stone arches, a tin soldier's castle. Our voices were truncated by the heavy snow, the stalactite icicles on the low roofs turned the town to a wintry cave; we spent most of our time in an echoing room lined with skis, because the professional there gave us a good feeling about the sports at which we were so inept. He was later taken up by the DuPonts on the same basis and made a powder magnate or something.

When we decided to go back to France we spent the night at the Pennsylvania, manipulating the new radio earphones and the servidors, where a suit can be frozen to a cube by nightfall. We were still impressed by running ice-water, self-sustaining rooms that could function even if besieged with current events. We were so little in touch with the world that they gave us an impression of a crowded subway station.

The hotel in Paris was triangular-shaped and faced Saint-Germain-des-Près. On Sundays we sat at the Deux Magots and watched the people, devout as an opera chorus, enter the old doors, or else watched the French read newspapers. There were long conversations about the ballet over sauerkraut in Lipps, and blank recuperative hours over books and prints in the dank Allée Bonaparte.

Now the trips away had begun to be less fun. The next one to Brittany broke at Le Mans. The lethargic town was crumbling away, pulverized by the heat of the white hot summer and only travelling salesmen slid their chairs pre-emptorily about the uncarpeted dining room. Plane trees bordered the route to La Baule.

At the Palace in La Baule we felt raucous amidst so much chic restraint. Children bronzed on the bare blue-white beach while the tide went out so far as to leave them crabs and starfish to dig for in the sands.

1929

We went to America but didn't stay at hotels. When we got back to Europe we spent the first night at a sun-flushed hostelry, Bertolini's in Genoa. There was a green tile bath and a very attentive valet de chambre and there was ballet to practice, using the brass bedstead as a bar. It was good to see the brilliant flowers colliding in prismatic explosions over the terraced hillside and to feel ourselves foreigners again.

Reaching Nice, we went economically to the Beau Rivage, which offered many stained glass windows to the Mediterranean glare. It was spring and was brittly cold along the Promenade des Anglais, though the crowds moved persistently in a summer tempo. We admired the painted windows of the converted palaces on the Place

Gambetta. Walking at dusk, the voices fell seductively through the nebulous twilight inviting us to share the first stars, but we were busy. We went to the cheap ballets of the Casino on the jettée and rode almost to Villefranche for *Salade Niçoise* and a very special bouillabaisse.

In Paris we economized again in a not-yet-dried cement hotel, the name of which we've forgotten. It cost us a good deal, for we ate out every night to avoid starchy table d'hôtes. Sylvia Beach invited us to dinner and the talk was all of the people who had discovered Joyce; we called on friends in better hotels: Zoë Akins, who had sought the picturesque of the open fires at Foyot's, and Esther at the Port-Royal, who took us to see Romaine Brooks' studio, a glass enclosed square of heaven swung high above Paris.

Then southward again, and wasting the dinner hour in an argument about which hotel: there was one in Beaune where Ernest Hemingway had liked the trout. Finally we decided to drive all night, and we ate well in a stable court-yard facing a canal—the green-white glare of Provence had already begun to dazzle us so that we didn't care whether the food was good or not. That night we stopped under the white-trunked trees to open the windshield to the moon and to the sweep of the south against our faces, and to better smell the fragrance rustling restlessly amidst the poplars.

At Fréjus Plage, they had built a new hotel, a barren structure facing the beach where the sailors bathe. We felt very superior remembering how we had been the first travellers to like the place in summer.

After the swimming at Cannes was over and the year's octopi had grown up in the crevices of the rocks, we started back to Paris. The night of the stock-market crash we stayed at the Beau Rivage in St. Raphaël in the room Ring Lardner had occupied another year. We got out as soon as we could because we had been there so many times before—it is sadder to find the past again and find it inadequate to the present than it is to have it elude you and remain forever a harmonious conception of memory.

At the Jules César in Arles we had a room that had once been a chapel. Following the festering waters of a stagnant canal we came to the ruins of a Roman dwelling-house. There was a blacksmith shop installed behind the proud columns and a few scattered cows ate the gold flowers off the meadow.

Then up and up; the twilit heavens expanded in the Cévennes valley, cracking the mountains apart, and there was a fearsome loneliness brooding on the flat tops. We crunched chestnut burrs on the road and aromatic smoke wound out of the mountain cottages. The Inn looked bad, the floors were covered with sawdust, but they gave us the best pheasant we ever ate and the best sausage, and the feather-beds were wonderful.

In Vichy, the leaves had covered the square about the wooden bandstand. Health advice was printed on the doors at the Hôtel du Parc and on the menu, but the salon was filled with people drinking champagne. We loved the massive trees in Vichy and the way the friendly town nestles in a hollow.

By the time we got to Tours, we had begun to feel like Cardinal Balue in his cage in the little Renault. The Hôtel de l'Univers was equally stuffy but after dinner we found a café crowded with people playing checkers and singing choruses and we felt we could go on to Paris after all.

Our cheap hotel in Paris had been turned into a girls' school—we went to a nameless one in the Rue du Bac, where potted palms withered in the exhausted air. Through the thin partitions we witnessed the private lives and natural functions of our neighbors. We walked at night past the moulded columns of the Odéon and identified the gangrenous statue behind the Luxembourg fence as Catherine de Medici.

It was a trying winter and to forget bad times we went to Algiers. The Hôtel de l'Oasis was laced together by Moorish grills; and the bar was an outpost of civilization with people accentuating their eccentricities. Beggars in white sheets were propped against the walls, and the dash of colonial uniforms gave the cafés a desperate swash-buckling air. Berbers have plaintive trusting eyes but it is really Fate they trust.

In Bou Saada, the scent of amber was swept along the streets by wide desert cloaks. We watched the moon stumble over the sand hillocks in a dead white glow and believed the guide as he told us of a priest he knew who could wreck railroad trains by wishing. The Ouled Naïls were very brown and clean-cut girls, impersonal as they turned themselves into fitting instruments for sex by the ritual of their dance, jangling their gold to the tune of savage fidelities hid in the distant hills.

The world crumbled to pieces in Biskra; the streets crept through the town like streams of hot white lava. Arabs sold nougat and cakes of poisonous pink under the flare of open gas jets. Since *The Garden of Allah* and *The Sheik* the town has been filled with frustrate women. In the steep cobbled alleys we flinched at the brightness of mutton carcases swung from the butchers' booths.

We stopped in El Kantara at a rambling inn whiskered with wistaria. Purple dusk steamed up from the depths of a gorge and we walked to a painter's house, where, in the remoteness of those mountains, he worked at imitations of Meissonier.

Then Switzerland and another life. Spring bloomed in the gardens of the Grand Hôtel in Glion, and a panorama world scintillated in the mountain air. The sun steamed delicate blossoms loose from the rocks while far below glinted the lake of Geneva.

Beyond the balustrade of the Lausanne Palace, sailboats plume themselves in the breeze like birds. Willow trees weave lacy patterns on the gravel terrace. The people are chic fugitives from life and death, rattling their teacups in querulous emotion on the deep protective balcony. They spell the names of hotels and cities with flowerbeds and laburnum in Switzerland and even the street lights wore crowns of verbena.

1931

Leisurely men played checkers in the restaurant of the Hôtel de la Paix in Lausanne. The depression had become frank in the American papers so we wanted to get back home.

But we went to Annecy for two weeks in summer, and said at the end that we'd never go there again because those weeks had been perfect and no other time could match them. First we lived at the Beau-Rivage, a rambler rose-covered hotel, with a diving platform wedged beneath our window between the sky and the lake, but there were enormous flies on the raft so we moved across the lake to Menthon. The water was greener there and the shadows long and cool and the scraggly gardens staggered up the shelved precipice to the Hôtel Palace. We played tennis on the baked clay courts and fished tentatively from a low brick wall. The heat of summer seethed in the resin of the white pine bath-houses. We walked at night towards a café blooming with Japanese lanterns, white shoes gleaming like radium in the damp darkness. It was like the good gone times when we still believed in summer hotels and the philosophies of popular songs. Another night we danced a Wiener waltz, and just simply swep' around.

At the Caux Palace, a thousand yards in the air, we tea-danced on the uneven boards of a pavilion and sopped our toast in mountain honey.

When we passed through Munich the Regina-Palast

was empty; they gave us a suite where the princes stayed in the days when royalty travelled. The young Germans stalking the ill-lit streets wore a sinister air—the talk that underscored the beer-garden waltzes was of war and hard times. Thornton Wilder took us to a famous restaurant where the beer deserved the silver mugs it was served in. We went to see the cherished witnesses to a lost cause; our voices echoed through the planetarium and we lost our orientation in the deep blue cosmic presentation of how things are.

In Vienna, the Bristol was the best hotel and they were glad to have us because it, too, was empty. Our windows looked out on the mouldy baroque of the Opera over the tops of sorrowing elms. We dined at the widow Sacher's— over the oak panelling hung a print of Franz Joseph going some happier place many years ago in a coach; one of the Rothschilds dined behind a leather screen. The city was poor already, or still, and the faces about us were harassed and defensive.

We stayed a few days at the Vevey Palace on Lake Geneva. The trees in the hotel gardens were the tallest we had ever seen and gigantic lonely birds fluttered over the surface of the lake. Farther along there was a gay little beach with a modern bar where we sat on the sands and discussed Stomachs.

We motored back to Paris: that is, we sat nervously in our six horse-power Renault. At the famous Hôtel de la Cloche in Dijon we had a nice room with a very complicated mechanical inferno of a bath, which the valet proudly referred to as American plumbing.

In Paris for the last time, we installed ourselves amidst the faded grandeurs of the Hôtel Majestic. We went to the Exposition and yielded up our imaginations to gold-lit facsimiles of Bali. Lonely flooded rice fields of lonely far-off islands told us an immutable story of work and death. The juxtaposition of so many replicas of so many civilizations was confusing, and depressing.

Back in America we stayed at the New Yorker because the advertisements said it was cheap. Everywhere quietude was sacrificed to haste and, momentarily, it seemed an impossible world, even though lustrous from the roof in the blue dusk.

In Alabama, the streets were sleepy and remote and a calliope on parade gasped out the tunes of our youth. There was sickness in the family and the house was full of nurses so we stayed at the big new elaborate Jefferson Davis. The old houses near the business section were falling to pieces at last. New bungalows lined the cedar drives on the outskirts; four-o'clocks bloomed beneath the old iron deer and arborvitae boxed the prim brick walks while vigorous weeds uprooted the pavements. Nothing had happened there since the Civil War. Everybody had forgotten why the hotel had been erected, and the clerk gave us three rooms and four baths for nine dollars a day. We used one as a sitting-room so the bell-boys would have some place to sleep when we rang for them.

1932

At the biggest hotel in Biloxi we read *Genesis* and watched the sea pave the deserted shore with a mosaic of black twigs.

We went to Florida. The bleak marshes were punctuated by biblical admonitions to a better life; abandoned fishing boats disintegrated in the sun. The Don Cesar Hotel in Pass-A-Grille stretched lazily over the stubbed wilderness, surrendering its shape to the blinding brightness of the gulf. Opalescent shells cupped the twilight on the beach and a stray dog's footprints in the wet sand staked out his claim to a free path round the ocean. We walked at night and discussed the Pythagorean theory of numbers, and we fished by day. We were sorry for the deep-sea bass and the amber-jacks—they seemed such easy game and no sport at all. Reading the *Seven Against Thebes*, we browned on a lonely beach. The hotel was almost empty and there were so many waiters waiting to be off that we could hardly eat our meals.

1933

The room in the Algonquin was high up amidst the gilded domes of New York. Bells chimed hours that had yet to penetrate the shadowy streets of the canyon. It was too hot in the room, but the carpets were soft and the room was isolated by dark corridors outside the door and bright façades outside the window. We spent much time getting ready for theatres. We saw Georgia O'Keefe's pictures and it was a deep emotional experience to abandon oneself to that majestic aspiration so adequately fitted into eloquent abstract forms.

For years we had wanted to go to Bermuda. We went. The Elbow Beach Hotel was full of honeymooners, who scintillated so persistently in each other's eyes that we cynically moved. The Hotel St. George was nice. Bougainvillea cascaded down the tree trunks and long stairs passed by deep mysteries taking place behind native windows. Cats slept along the balustrade and lovely children grew. We rode bicycles along the wind-swept causeways and stared in a dreamy daze at such phenomena as roosters scratching amidst the sweet alyssum. We drank sherry on a veranda above the bony backs of horses tethered in the public square. We had travelled a lot, we thought. Maybe this would be the last trip for a long while. We thought Bermuda was a nice place to be the last one of so many years of travelling.

Sleeping and Waking

December, 1934

WHEN SOME YEARS AGO I read a piece by Ernest Hemingway called *Now I Lay Me,* I thought there was nothing further to be said about insomnia. I see now that that was because I had never had much; it appears that every man's insomnia is as different from his neighbor's as are their daytime hopes and aspirations.

Now if insomnia is going to be one of your naturals, it begins to appear in the late thirties. Those seven precious hours of sleep suddenly break in two. There is, if one is lucky, the "first sweet sleep of night" and the last deep sleep of morning, but between the two appears a sinister, ever widening interval. This is the time of which it is written in the Psalms: *Scuto circumdabit te veritas eius: non timebis a timore nocturno, a sagitta volante in die, a negotio perambulante in tenebris.*

With a man I knew the trouble commenced with a mouse; in my case I like to trace it to a single mosquito.

My friend was in course of opening up his country house unassisted, and after a fatiguing day discovered that the only practical bed was a child's affair—long enough but scarcely wider than a crib. Into this he flopped and was presently deeply engrossed in rest *but* with one arm irrepressibly extending over the side of the crib. Hours later he was awakened by what seemed to be a pin-prick in his finger. He shifted his arm sleepily and dozed off again—to be again awakened by the same feeling.

This time he flipped on the bed-light—and there attached to the bleeding end of his finger was a small and avid mouse. My friend, to use his own words, "uttered an exclamation," but probably he gave a wild scream.

The mouse let go. It had been about the business of devouring the man as thoroughly as if his sleep were permanent. From then on it threatened to be not even temporary. The victim sat shivering, and very, very tired. He considered how he would have a cage made to fit over the bed and sleep under it the rest of his life. But it was too late to have the cage made that night and finally he dozed, to wake in intermittent horrors from dreams of being a Pied Piper whose rats turned about and pursued him.

He has never since been able to sleep without a dog or cat in the room.

My own experience with night pests was at a time of utter exhaustion—too much work undertaken, interlocking circumstances that made the work twice as arduous, illness within and around—the old story of troubles never coming singly. And ah, how I had planned that sleep that was to crown the end of the struggle—how I had looked forward to the relaxation into a bed soft as a cloud and permanent as a grave. An invitation to dine *à deux* with

Greta Garbo would have left me indifferent.

But had there been such an invitation I would have done well to accept it, for instead I dined alone, or rather was dined upon by one solitary mosquito.

It is astonishing how much worse one mosquito can be than a swarm. A swarm can be prepared against, but *one* mosquito takes on a personality—a hatefulness, a sinister quality of the struggle to the death. This personality appeared all by himself in September on the twentieth floor of a New York hotel, as out of place as an armadillo. He was the result of New Jersey's decreased appropriation for swamp drainage, which had sent him and other younger sons into neighboring states for food.

The night was warm—but after the first encounter the vague slappings of the air, the futile searches, the punishment of my own ears a split second too late, I followed the ancient formula and drew the sheet over my head.

And so there continued the old story, the bitings through the sheet, the sniping of exposed sections of hand holding the sheet in place, the pulling up of the blanket with ensuing suffocation—followed by the psychological change of attitude, increasing wakefulness, wild impotent anger—finally a second hunt.

This inaugurated the maniacal phase—the crawl under the bed with the standing lamp for torch, the tour of the room with final detection of the insect's retreat on the ceiling and attack with knotted towels, the wounding of oneself—my God!

—After that there was a short convalescence that my

opponent seemed aware of, for he perched insolently be-
side my head—but I missed again.

At last, after another half hour that whipped the nerves
into a frantic state of alertness came the Pyrrhic victory,
and the small mangled spot of blood, *my* blood, on the
head-board of the bed.

As I said, I think of that night, two years ago, as the
beginning of my sleeplessness—because it gave me the
sense of how sleep can be spoiled by one infinitesimal
incalculable element. It made me, in the now archaic
phraseology, "sleep-conscious." I worried whether or not
it was going to be allowed me. I was drinking, intermit-
tently but generously, and on the nights when I took no
liquor the problem of whether or not sleep was specified
began to haunt me long before bedtime.

A typical night (and I wish I could say such nights were
all in the past) comes after a particularly sedentary work-
and-cigarette day. It ends, say, without any relaxing interval, at the time for going to bed. All is prepared, the
books, the glass of water, the extra pajamas lest I awake
in rivulets of sweat, the luminol pills in the little round
tube, the note book and pencil in case of a night thought
worth recording. (Few have been—they generally seem
thin in the morning, which does not diminish their force
and urgency at night.)

I turn in, perhaps with a night-cap—I am doing some
comparatively scholarly reading for a coincident work
so I choose a lighter volume on the subject and read till
drowsy on a last cigarette. At the yawning point I snap the

book on a marker, the cigarette at the hearth, the button on the lamp. I turn first on the left side, for that, so I've heard, slows the heart, and then—coma.

So far so good. From midnight until two-thirty peace in the room. Then suddenly I am awake, harassed by one of the ills or functions of the body, a too vivid dream, a change in the weather for warm or cold.

The adjustment is made quickly, with the vain hope that the continuity of sleep can be preserved, but no—so with a sigh I flip on the light, take a minute pill of luminol and reopen my book. The *real* night, the darkest hour, has begun. I am too tired to read unless I get myself a drink and hence feel bad next day—so I get up and walk. I walk from my bedroom through the hall to my study, and then back again, and if it's summer out to my back porch. There is a mist over Baltimore; I cannot count a single steeple. Once more to the study, where my eye is caught by a pile of unfinished business; letters, proofs, notes, etc. I start toward it, but No! this would be fatal. Now the luminol is having some slight effect, so I try bed again, this time half circling the pillow on edge about my neck.

"Once upon a time" (I tell myself) "they needed a quarterback at Princeton, and they had nobody and were in despair. The head coach noticed me kicking and passing on the side of the field, and he cried: 'Who is *that* man—why haven't we noticed *him* before?' The under coach answered, 'He hasn't been out,' and the response was: 'Bring him to me.'

" … we go to the day of the Yale game. I weigh only one

hundred and thirty-five, so they save me until the third quarter, with the score—"

—But it's no use—I have used that dream of a defeated dream to induce sleep for almost twenty years, but it has worn thin at last. I can no longer count on it—though even now on easier nights it has a certain lull ...

The war dream then: the Japanese are everywhere victorious—my division is cut to rags and stands on the defensive in a part of Minnesota where I know every bit of the ground. The headquarters staff and the regimental battalion commanders who were in conference with them at the time have been killed by one shell. The command devolved upon Captain Fitzgerald. With superb presence ...

—but enough; this also is worn thin with years of usage. The character who bears my name has become blurred. In the dead of the night I am only one of the dark millions, riding forward in black buses toward the unknown.

Back again now to the rear porch, and conditioned by intense fatigue of mind and perverse alertness of the nervous system—like a broken-stringed bow upon a throbbing fiddle—I see the real horror develop over the rooftops, and in the strident horns of night-owl taxis and the shrill monody of revelers' arrival over the way. Horror and waste—

—Waste and horror—what I might have been and done that is lost, spent, gone, dissipated, unrecapturable. I could have acted thus, refrained from this, been bold where I was timid, cautious where I was rash.

I need not have hurt her like that.

Nor said this to him.

Nor broken myself trying to break what was unbreakable.

The horror has come now like a storm—what if this night prefigured the night after death—what if all thereafter was an eternal quivering on the edge of an abyss, with everything base and vicious in oneself urging one forward and the baseness and viciousness of the world just ahead. No choice, no road, no hope—only the endless repetition of the sordid and the semi-tragic. Or to stand forever, perhaps, on the threshold of life unable to pass it and return to it. I am a ghost now as the clock strikes four.

On the side of the bed I put my head in my hands. Then silence, silence—and suddenly—or so it seems in retrospect—suddenly I am asleep.

Sleep—real sleep, the dear, the cherished one, the lullaby. So deep and warm the bed and the pillow enfolding me, letting me sink into peace, nothingness—my dreams now, after the catharsis of the dark hours, are of young and lovely people doing young, lovely things, the girls I knew once, with big brown eyes, real yellow hair.

In the fall of '16 in the cool of the afternoon
I met Caroline under a white moon
There was an orchestra—Bingo-Bango
Playing for us to dance the tango
And the people all clapped as we arose
For her sweet face and my new clothes—

Life *was* like that, after all; my spirit soars in the moment of its oblivion; then down, down deep into the pillow...

" ... Yes, Essie, yes.—Oh, My God, all right, I'll take the call myself."

Irresistible, iridescent—here is Aurorar—here is another day.

My Lost City

THERE WAS FIRST the ferry boat moving softly from the Jersey shore at dawn—the moment crystallized into my first symbol of New York. Five years later when I was fifteen I went into the city from school to see Ina Claire in *The Quaker Girl* and Gertrude Bryan in *Little Boy Blue*. Confused by my hopeless and melancholy love for them both, I was unable to choose between them—so they blurred into one lovely entity, the girl. She was my second symbol of New York. The ferry boat stood for triumph, the girl for romance. In time I was to achieve some of both, but there was a third symbol that I have lost somewhere, and lost forever.

I found it on a dark April afternoon after five more years.

"Oh, Bunny," I yelled. "*Bunny!*"

He did not hear me—my taxi lost him, picked him up again half a block down the street There were black spots of rain on the sidewalk and I saw him walking briskly through the crowd wearing a tan raincoat over his inevitable brown get-up; I noted with a shock that he was carrying a light cane.

"Bunny!" I called again, and stopped. I was still an undergraduate at Princeton while he had become a New Yorker.

This was his afternoon walk, this hurry along with his stick through the gathering rain, and as I was not to meet him for an hour it seemed an intrusion to happen upon him engrossed in his private life. But the taxi kept pace with him and as I continued to watch I was impressed: he was no longer the shy little scholar of Holder Court—he walked with confidence, wrapped in his thoughts and looking straight ahead, and it was obvious that his new background was entirely sufficient to him. I knew that he had an apartment where he lived with three other men, released now from all undergraduate taboos, but there was something else that was nourishing him and I got my first impression of that new thing—the Metropolitan spirit.

Up to this time I had seen only the New York that offered itself for inspection—I was Dick Whittington up from the country gaping at the trained bears, or a youth of the Midi dazzled by the boulevards of Paris. I had come only to stare at the show, though the designers of the Woolworth Building and the Chariot Race Sign, the producers of musical comedies and problem plays, could ask for no more appreciative spectator, for I took the style and glitter of New York even above its own valuation. But I had never accepted any of the practically anonymous invitations to debutante balls that turned up in an undergraduate's mail, perhaps because I felt that no actuality could live up to my conception of New York's splendor. Moreover, she to whom I fatuously referred as "my girl" was a Middle Westerner, a fact which kept the warm center of the world out there, so I thought of New York as essentially cynical and heartless—save for one night when she made luminous the Ritz Roof on a brief passage through.

Lately, however, I had definitely lost her and I wanted a man's world, and this sight of Bunny made me see New York as just that. A week before, Monsignor Fay had taken me to the Lafayette where there was spread before us a brilliant flag of food, called an *hors d'oeuvre*, and with it we drank claret that was as brave as Bunny's confident cane—but after all it was a restaurant, and afterwards we would drive back over a bridge into the hinterland. The New York of undergraduate dissipation, of Bustanoby's, Shanley's, Jack's, had become a horror, and though I returned to it, alas, through many an alcoholic mist, I felt each time a betrayal of a persistent idealism. My participance was prurient rather than licentious and scarcely one pleasant memory of it remains from those days; as Ernest Hemingway once remarked, the sole purpose of the cabaret is for unattached men to find complaisant women. All the rest is a wasting of time in bad air.

But that night, in Bunny's apartment, life was mellow and safe, a finer distillation of all that I had come to love at Princeton. The gentle playing of an oboe mingled with city noises from the street outside, which penetrated into the room with difficulty through great barricades of books; only the crisp tearing open of invitations by one man was a discordant note. I had found a third symbol of New York and I began wondering about the rent of such apartments and casting about for the appropriate friends to share one with me.

Fat chance—for the next two years I had as much control over my own destiny as a convict over the cut of his clothes. When I got back to New York in 1919 I was so entangled in life that a period of mellow monasticism in Washington Square was not to be dreamed of. The thing was to make enough money in the advertising business to rent a stuffy apartment for two in the Bronx. The girl concerned had never seen New York but she was wise enough to be rather reluctant. And in a haze of anxiety and unhappiness I passed the four most impressionable months of my life.

New York had all the iridescence of the beginning of the world. The returning troops marched up Fifth Avenue and girls were instinctively drawn East and North toward them—this was the greatest nation and there was gala in the air. As I hovered ghost-like in the Plaza Red Room of a Saturday afternoon, or went to lush and liquid garden parties in the East Sixties or tippled with Princetonians in the Biltmore Bar I was haunted always by my other life— my drab room in the Bronx, my square foot of the subway, my fixation upon the day's letter from Alabama— would it come and what would it say?—my shabby suits, my poverty, and love. While my friends were launching decently into life I had muscled my inadequate bark into midstream. The gilded youth circling around young Constance Bennett in the Club de Vingt, the classmates in the Yale-Princeton Club whooping up our first after-the-war reunion, the atmosphere of the millionaires' houses that I sometimes frequented—these things were empty for me, though I recognized them as impressive scenery and regretted that I was committed to other romance. The most hilarious luncheon table or the most moony cabaret—it was all the same; from them I returned eagerly to my home on Claremont Avenue—home because there might be a letter waiting outside the door. One by one my great dreams of New York became tainted. The remembered charm of Bunny's apartment faded with the rest when I interviewed a blowsy landlady in Greenwich Village. She told me I could bring girls to the room, and the idea filled me with dismay—why should I want to bring girls to my room?—I had a girl. I wandered through the town of 127th Street, resenting its vibrant life; or else I bought cheap theatre seats at Gray's drugstore and tried to lose myself for a few hours in my old passion for Broadway. I was a failure—mediocre at advertising work and unable to get started as a writer. Hating the city, I got roaring, weeping drunk on my last penny and went home....

... Incalculable city. What ensued was only one of a thousand success stories of those gaudy days, but it plays a part in my own movie of New York. When I returned six months later the offices of editors and publishers were open to me, impresarios begged plays, the movies panted for screen material. To my bewilderment, I was adopted, not as a Middle Westerner, not even as a detached observer, but as the archetype of what New York wanted. This statement requires some account of the metropolis in 1920.

There was already the tall white city of today, already the feverish activity of the boom, but there was a general inarticulateness. As much as anyone the columnist F. P. A. guessed the pulse of the individual and the crowd, but shyly, as one watching from a window. Society and the native arts had not mingled—Ellen Mackay was not yet married to Irving Berlin. Many of Peter Arno's people would have been meaningless to the citizen of 1920, and save for F. P. A.'s column there was no forum for metropolitan urbanity.

Then, for just a moment, the "younger generation" idea became a fusion of many elements in New York life. People of fifty might pretend there was still a four hundred, or Maxwell Bodenheim might pretend there was a Bohemia worth its paint and pencils—but the blending of the bright, gay, vigorous elements began then, and for the first time there appeared a society a little livelier than the solid mahogany dinner parties of Emily Price Post. If this society produced the cocktail party, it also evolved Park Avenue wit, and for the first time an educated European could envisage a trip to New York as something more amusing than a gold-trek into a formalized Australian Bush.

For just a moment, before it was demonstrated that I was unable to play the role, I, who knew less of New York then any reporter of six months standing and less of its society than any hall-room boy in a Ritz stag line, was pushed into the position not only of spokesman for the time but of the typical product of that same moment. I, or rather it was "we" now, did not know exactly what New York expected of us and found it rather confusing. Within a few months after our embarkation on the Metropolitan venture we scarcely knew any more who we were and we hadn't a notion what we were. A dive into a civic fountain, a casual brush with the law, was enough to get us into the gossip columns, and we were quoted on a variety of subjects we knew nothing about. Actually our "contacts" included half a dozen unmarried college friends and a few new literary acquaintances—I remember a lonesome Christmas when we had not one friend in the city, nor one house we could go to. Finding no nucleus to which we could cling, we became a small nucleus ourselves and gradually we fitted our disruptive personalities into the contemporary scene of New York. Or rather New York forgot us and let us stay.

This is not an account of the city's changes but of the changes in this writer's feeling for the city. From the confusion of the year 1920 I remember riding on top of a taxicab along deserted Fifth Avenue on a hot Sunday night, and a luncheon in the cool Japanese gardens at the Ritz with the wistful Kay Laurel and George Jean Nathan, and writing all night again and again, and paying too much for minute apartments, and buying magnificent but broken-down cars. The first speakeasies had arrived, the toddle was passe, the Montmartre was the smart place to dance and Lillian Tashman's fair hair weaved around the floor among the enliquored college boys. The plays were *Declassée* and *Sacred and Profane Love*, and at the Midnight Frolic you danced elbow to elbow with Marion Davies and perhaps picked out the vivacious Mary Hay in the pony chorus. We thought we were apart from all that;

perhaps everyone thinks they are apart from their milieu. We felt like small children in a great bright unexplored barn. Summoned out to Griffith's studio on Long Island, we trembled in the presence of the familiar faces of the *Birth of a Nation*; later I realized that behind much of the entertainment that the city poured forth into the nation there were only a lot of rather lost and lonely people. The world of the picture actors was like our own in that it was in New York and not of it. It had little sense of itself and no center: when I first met Dorothy Gish I had the feeling that we were both standing on the North Pole and it was snowing. Since then they have found a home but it was not destined to be New York.

When bored we took our city with a Huysmans-like perversity. An afternoon alone in our "apartment" eating olive sandwiches and drinking a quart of Bushmill's whiskey presented by Zoë Akins, then out into the freshly bewitched city, through strange doors into strange apartments with intermittent swings along in taxis through the soft nights. At last we were one with New York, pulling it after us through every portal. Even now I go into many flats with the sense that I have been there before or in the one above or below—was it the night I tried to disrobe in the *Scandals,* or the night when (as I read with astonishment in the paper next morning) "Fitzgerald Knocks Officer This Side of Paradise"? Successful scrapping not being among my accomplishments, I tried in vain to reconstruct the sequence of events which led up to this dénouement in Webster Hall. And lastly from that period I remember riding in a taxi one afternoon between very tall buildings under a mauve and rosy sky; I began to bawl because I had everything I wanted and knew I would never be so happy again.

It was typical of our precarious position in New York that when our child was to be born we played safe and went home to St. Paul—it seemed inappropriate to bring a baby into all that glamor and loneliness. But in a year we were back and we began doing the same things over again and not liking them so much. We had run through a lot, though we had retained an almost theatrical innocence by preferring the role of the observed to that of the observer. But innocence is no end in itself and as our minds unwillingly matured we began to see New York whole and try to save some of it for the selves we would inevitably become.

It was too late—or too soon. For us the city was inevitably linked up with Bacchic diversions, mild or fantastic. We could organize ourselves only on our return to Long Island and not always there. We had no incentive to meet the city half way. My first symbol was now a memory, for I knew that triumph is in oneself; my second one had grown commonplace—two of the actresses whom I had worshipped from afar in 1913 had dined in our house. But it filled me with a certain fear that even the third symbol had grown dim—the tranquillity of Bunny's apartment was not to be found in the ever-quickening city. Bunny himself was married, and about to become a father, other friends had gone to Europe, and the bachelors had become cadets of houses larger and more social than ours.

By this time we "knew everybody"—which is to say most of those whom Ralph Barton would draw as in the orchestra on an opening night

But we were no longer important. The flapper, upon whose activities the popularity of my first books was based, had become *passé* by 1923—anyhow in the East. I decided to crash Broadway with a play, but Broadway sent its scouts to Atlantic City and quashed the idea in advance, so I felt that for the moment, the city and I had little to offer each other. I would take the Long Island atmosphere that I had familiarly breathed and materialize it beneath unfamiliar skies.

It was three years before we saw New York again. As the ship glided up the river, the city burst thunderously upon us in the early dusk—the white glacier of lower New York swooping down like a strand of a bridge to rise into uptown New York, a miracle of foamy light suspended by the stars. A band started to play on deck, but the majesty of the city made the march trivial and tinkling. From that moment I knew that New York, however often I might leave it, was home.

The tempo of the city had changed sharply. The uncertainties of 1920 were drowned in a steady golden roar and many of our friends had grown wealthy. But the restlessness of New York in 1927 approached hysteria. The parties were bigger—those of Condé Nast, for example, rivaled in their way the fabled balls of the nineties; the pace was faster—the catering to dissipation set an example to Paris; the shows were broader, the buildings were higher, the morals were looser and the liquor was cheaper; but all these benefits did not really minister to much delight. Young people wore out early—they were hard and languid at twenty-one, and save for Peter Arno none of them contributed anything new; perhaps Peter Arno and his collaborators said everything there was to say about the boom days in New York that couldn't be said by a jazz band. Many people who were not alcoholics were lit up four days out of seven, and frayed nerves were strewn everywhere; groups were held together by a generic nervousness and the hangover became a part of the day as well allowed-for as the Spanish siesta. Most of my friends drank too much—the more they were in tune to the times the more they drank. And as effort *per se* had no dignity against the mere bounty of those days in New York, a depreciatory word was found for it: a successful programme became a racket—I was in the literary racket.

We settled a few hours from New York and I found that every time I came to the city I was caught up into a complication of events that deposited me a few days later in a somewhat exhausted state on the train for Delaware. Whole sections of the city had grown rather poisonous, but invariably I found a moment of utter peace in riding south through Central Park at dark towards where the façade of 59th Street thrusts its lights through the trees. There again was my lost city, wrapped cool in its mystery and promise. But that detachment never lasted long—as the toiler must live in the city's belly, so I was compelled to live in its disordered mind.

Instead there were the speakeasies—the moving from luxurious bars, which advertised in the campus publications of Yale and Princeton, to the beer gardens where the snarling face of the underworld peered through the German good nature of the entertainment, then on to strange and even more sinister localities where one was eyed by granite-faced boys and there was nothing left of joviality but only a brutishness that corrupted the new day into which one presently went out. Back in 1920 I shocked a rising young business man by suggesting a cocktail before lunch. In 1929 there was liquor in half the downtown offices, and a speakeasy in half the large buildings.

One was increasingly conscious of the speakeasy and of Park Avenue. In the past decade Greenwich Village, Washington Square, Murray Hill, the châteaux of Fifth Avenue had somehow disappeared, or become unexpressive of anything. The city was bloated, gutted, stupid with cake and circuses, and a new expression "Oh yeah?" summed up all the enthusiasm evoked by the announcement of the last super-skyscrapers. My barber retired on a half million bet in the market and I was conscious that the head waiters who bowed me, or failed to bow me, to my table were far, far wealthier than I. This was no fun—once again I had enough of New York and it was good to be safe on shipboard where the ceaseless revelry remained in the bar in transport to the fleecing rooms of France.

"What news from New York?"

"Stocks go up. A baby murdered a gangster."

"Nothing more?"

"Nothing. Radios blare in the street."

I once thought that there were no second acts in American lives, but there was certainly to be a second act to New York's boom days. We were somewhere in North Africa when we heard a dull distant crash which echoed to the farthest wastes of the desert.

"What was that?"

"Did you hear it?"

"It was nothing."

"Do you think we ought to go home and see?"

"No—it was nothing."

In the dark autumn of two years later we saw New York again. We passed through curiously polite customs agents, and then with bowed head and hat in hand I walked reverently through the echoing tomb. Among the ruins a few childish wraiths still played to keep up the pretense that they were alive, betraying by their feverish voices and hectic cheeks the thinness of the masquerade. Cocktail parties, a last hollow survival from the days of carnival, echoed to the plaints of the wounded: "Shoot me, for the love of God, someone shoot me!", and the groans and wails of the dying: "Did you see that United States Steel is down three more points?" My barber was back at work in his shop; again the head waiters bowed people to their tables, if there were people to be bowed. From the ruins, lonely and inexplicable as the sphinx, rose the Empire State Building and, just as it had been a tradition of mine to climb to the Plaza Roof to take leave of the beautiful city, extending as far as eyes could reach, so now

I went to the roof of the last and most magnificent of towers. Then I understood—everything was explained: I had discovered the crowning error of the city, its Pandora's box. Full of vaunting pride the New Yorker had climbed here and seen with dismay what he had never suspected, that the city was not the endless succession of canyons that he had supposed but that *it had limits*—from the tallest structure he saw for the first time that it faded out into the country on all sides, into an expanse of green and blue that alone was limitless. And with the awful realization that New York was a city after all and not a universe, the whole shining edifice that he had reared in his imagination came crashing to the ground. That was the rash gift of Alfred W. Smith to the citizens of New York.

Thus I take leave of my lost city. Seen from the ferry boat in the early morning, it no longer whispers of fantastic success and eternal youth. The whoopee mamas who prance before its empty parquets do not suggest to me the ineffable beauty of my dream girls of 1914. And Bunny, swinging along confidently with his cane toward his cloister in a carnival, has gone over to Communism and frets about the wrongs of southern mill workers and western farmers whose voices, fifteen years ago, would not have penetrated his study walls.

All is lost save memory, yet sometimes I imagine myself reading, with curious interest, a *Daily News* of the issue of 1945:

MAN OF FIFTY RUNS AMUCK IN NEW YORK

*Fitzgerald Feathered Many Love Nests Cutie Avers
Bumped Off By Outraged Gunman*

So perhaps I am destined to return some day and find in the city new experiences that so far I have only read about. For the moment I can only cry out that I have lost my splendid mirage. Come back, come back, O glittering and white!

Selections from the Letters

To Edmund Wilson

> [1920]
> 599 Summit Ave.
> St. Paul, Minn
> August 15th

Dear Bunny:

Delighted to get your letter. I am deep in the throes of a new novel.

Which is the best title

(1) *The Education of a Personage*

(2) *The Romantic Egotist*

(3) *This Side of Paradise*

I am sending it to Scribner. They liked my first one. Am enclosing two letters from them that might amuse you. Please return them.

I have just finished up the story for your book. It's not written yet. An American girl falls in love with an officer Francais at a southern camp.

Since I last saw you I've tried to get married & then tried

to drink myself to death but foiled, as have so many good men, by the sex and the state I have returned to literature.

Have sold three or four cheap stories to American magazines.

Will start on story for you about 25th d'Auout (as the French say or do not say) (which is about 10 days off)

I am ashamed to say that my Catholicism is scarcely more than a memory—no that's wrong it's more than that; at any rate I do not go to the church nor mumble stray nothings over chrystaline beads.

Maybe in N'York in Sept or early Oct.

Is John Bishop in hoc terrain? ...

For God's sake Bunny write a novel & don't waste your time editing collections. It'll get to be a habit.

That sounds crass & discordant but you know what I mean.

Yours in the Holder* group
Scott Fitzgerald

* This refers to Holder Hall, one of the Princeton dormitories

To John Peale Bishop

> [Winter of 1924–25]
> I am quite drunk
> I am told that this is Capri;
> though as I remember Capri
> was quieter

Dear John:

As the literary wits might say, your letter received and contents quoted. Let us have more of the same—I think it showed a great deal of power and the last scene—the dinner at the young Bishops—was handled with admirable restraint. I am glad that at last Americans are at last producing letters of their own. The climax was wonderful and the exquisite irony of the "sincerely yours" has only been equaled in the works of those two masters Flaubert and Ferber....

I will now have two copies of Westcott's *Apple* as in despair I ordered one—a regular orchard. I shall give one to Brooks whom I like. Do you know Brooks? He's just a fellow here....

Excuse the delay. I have been working on the envelope....

That was a caller. His name was Musselini, I think, and he says he is in politics here. And besides I have lost my pen and so I will have to continue writing in pencil* ... It turned up—I was writing with it all the time and hadn't noticed. That is because I am full of my new work, a historical play based on the life of Woodrow Wilson.

---

* This sentence is written in pencil. The rest of the letter is in ink.

Act I At Princeton

Woodrow seen teaching philosophy. Enter Pyne. Quarrel scene—Wilson refuses to recognize clubs. Enter woman with Bastard from Trenton. Pyne reenters with glee club and trustees. Noise outside "We have won—Princeton 12-Lafayette 3." Cheers. Football team enter and group around Wilson. Old Nassau. Curtain.

Act. II. Gubernatorial Mansion at Patterson

Wilson seen signing papers. Tasker Bliss and Marc Connelly come in with proposition to let bosses get control. "I have important papers to sign—and none of them legalize corruption." Triangle Club begins to sing outside window.... Enter women with Bastard from Trenton. President continues to sign papers. Enter Mrs. Galt, John Grier Hibben, Al Jolsen and Grantland Rice. Song "The call to Larger Duty." Tableau. Coughdrop.

Act III. (Optional)

The Battle front 1918

Act IV.

The peace congress. Clemenceau, Wilson and Jolsen at table.... The junior prom committee comes in through the skylight. Clemenceau: "We want the Sarre." Wilson: "No sarre, I won't hear of it." Laughter.... Enter Marylyn

Miller, Gilbert Seldes, and Irish Meusel. Tasker Bliss falls into cuspidor.

Oh Christ! I'm sobering up! Write me the opinion you may be pleased to form of my chef d'oevre and others opinion. *Please!* I think it's great but because it deals with much debauched materials, quick-deciders like Rasco may mistake it for Chambers. To me it's fascinating. I never get tired of it....

Zelda's been sick in bed for five weeks, poor child, and is only now looking up. No news except I now get 2000 a story and they grow worse and worse and my ambition is to get where I need write no more but only novels. Is Lewis' book any good? I imagine that mine is infinitely better—what else is well-reviewed this spring? Maybe my book* is rotten but I don't think so.

What are you writing? Please tell me something about your novel. And if I like the idea maybe I'll make it into a short story for the Post to appear just before your novel and steal the thunder. Who's going to do it? Bebé Daniels? She's a wow!

How was Townsend's first picture. Good reviews? What's Alec doing? And Ludlow? And Bunny? Did you read Ernest Boyd's account of what I might ironically call our "private" life in his *"Portraits?"* Did you like it? I rather did.

Scott

I am quite drunk again and enclose a postage stamp.

* *The Great Gatsby.*

F. Scott Fitzgerald

To John Peale Bishop

> [Probably January
> or February, 1929]
> % Guaranty Trust

Dear John:

My depression over the badness of the novel* as novel
had just about sunk me, when I began the novellette†—
John, it's like two different men writing. The novelette is
one of the best war things I've ever read—right up with
the very best of Crane and Bierce—intelligent, beautifully
organized and written—oh, it moved me and delighted
me—the Charlestown country, the night in town, the old
lady—but most of all, in the position I was in at 4 this
afternoon when I was in agony about the novel, the really fine dramatic handling of the old lady—and—silver
episode and the butchering scene. The preparation for the
latter was adroit and delicate and just enough.

Now, to be practical—*Scribner's Magazine* will, I'm sure,
publish the novelette, if you wish, and pay you 250–400
therefore. This price is a guess but probably accurate. I'd
be glad to act as your amateur agent in the case. It is *almost
impossible* without a big popular name to sell a two-part
story to any higher priced magazine than that, as I know
from my experience with *Diamond Big as the Ritz, Rich Boy*,
ect. Advise me as to whether I may go ahead—of course

* An unpublished novel by Bishop.
† *The Cellar*, a short story by Bishop.

authority confined only to American serial rights.

The novel is just something you've learned from and profited by. It has occasional spurts—like the conversations frequently of Brakespeare, but it is terribly tepid—I refrain—rather I don't refrain but here set down certain facts which you are undoubtedly quite aware of as I am....*

I'm taking you for a beating, but do you remember your letters to me about *Gatsby*. I suffered, but I got something like I did out of your friendly tutelage in English poetry.

A big person can make a much bigger mess than a little person and your impressive stature converted a lot of pottery during the three years or so you were in the works. Luckily the pottery was never very dear to you. Novels are not written, or at least begun with the idea of making an ultimate philosophical system—you tried to atone for your lack of confidence by a lack of humility before the form.

The main thing is: no one in our language possibly excepting Wilder has your talent for "the world," your culture and acuteness of social criticism as upheld by the story. There the approach (2nd and 3rd person ect) is considered, full scope in choice of subject for your special talents (descriptive power, sense of "le pays," ramifications of your special virtues such as loyalty, concealment of sensuality that is your bête noire to such an extent that you can no longer see it black, like me in my drunkenness.

Anyhow the story is marvellous. Don't be mad at this

---

* There follow several pages of detailed criticism of the novel, which can be of no interest to anyone but myself. J.P.B.

letter. I have the horrors tonight and perhaps am taking it out on you. Write me when I could see you here in Paris in the afternoon between 2.30 and 6.30 and talk—and name a day and a café at your convenience—I have no dates save on Sunday, so any day will suit me. Meanwhile I will make one more stab at your novel to see if I can think of anyway by a miracle of cutting it could be made more presentable. But I fear there's neither honor nor money in it for you

Your old and Always
Affectionate Friend
Scott

Excuse Christ-like tone of letter. Began tippling at page 2 and am now positively holy (like Dostoevsky's non-stinking monk)